A STUDY OF
PHILEMON, 2 JOHN,
3 JOHN, AND JUDE

NEW
TESTAMENT
POSTCARDS

From the Bible-teaching ministry of

CHARLES R.
SWINDOLL

INSIGHT FOR LIVING

Chuck graduated in 1963 from Dallas Theological Seminary, where he now serves as the school's fourth president, helping to prepare a new generation of men and women for the ministry. Chuck has served in pastorates in three states: Massachusetts, Texas, and California, including almost twenty-three years at the First Evangelical Free Church in Fullerton, California. His sermon messages have been aired over radio since 1979 as the *Insight for Living* broadcast. A best-selling author, Chuck has written numerous books and booklets on many subjects.

Based on the outlines and transcripts of Chuck's sermons, the study guide text is co-authored by Ken Gire, a graduate of Texas Christian University and Dallas Theological Seminary and Bryce Klabunde, a graduate of Biola University and Dallas Theological Seminary. Bryce Klabunde also wrote the Living Insights sections.

Editor in Chief:
Cynthia Swindoll

Coauthors of Text:
Ken Gire
Bryce Klabunde

Author of Living Insights:
Bryce Klabunde

Assistant Editor and Writer:
Wendy Peterson

Copy Editors:
Deborah Gibbs
Tom Kimber

Cover and Text Design:
Gary Lett

Graphics System Administrator:
Bob Haskins

Publishing System Specialist:
Alex Pasieka

Director, Communications Division:
John Norton

Marketing Manager:
Alene Cooper

Project Coordinator:
Colette Muse

Printer:
Sinclair Printing Company

Unless otherwise identified, all Scripture references are from the New American Standard Bible, © The Lockman Foundation 1960, 1962, 1963, 1968, 1971, 1972, 1973, 1975, 1977. Used by permission.

An effort has been made to locate sources and obtain permission where necessary for the quotations used in this book. In the event of any unintentional omission, a modification will gladly be incorporated in future printings.

ISBN 0-8499-8737-7
COVER PHOTOGRAPH: NEO Photo, Inc., Jack Fritze, Photographer
Printed in the United States of America

CONTENTS

INTRODUCTION

Postcards bring out our curious side, don't they? They beckon us to read them—the exotic stamp, the inviting photo of some faraway place, the tiny writing. And if they're addressed to someone else, our curiosity is really piqued. Anyone with an ounce of nosiness could never pass one up!

It's ironic, then, that of all the letters in the New Testament, the little one-chapter postcards are read the least. Perhaps the pages of our Bibles get stuck together, and we flip past them without realizing it. Or maybe, because they're so short, we think they're unimportant.

Well, these little missiles of truth pack a big punch. They're aimed at some pretty relevant issues: how our oneness in Christ transcends social boundaries, how to love with discernment, how to deal with false teachers who are wrecking the church, plus other equally significant issues.

Getting curious? Good! Even though they were addressed to someone else, they were written for all of us. So let's dig in!

Chuck Swindoll

Chuck Swindoll

PUTTING TRUTH INTO ACTION

K nowledge apart from application falls short of God's desire for His children. He wants us to apply what we learn so that we will change and grow. This study guide was prepared with these goals in mind. As you go through the following pages, we hope your desire to discover biblical truth will grow as your understanding of God's Word increases and that you will be encouraged to apply what you've learned.

To assist you in your study, we've included a section called ☀️**Living Insights** at the end of each lesson. These exercises will challenge you to study further and to think of specific ways to put your discoveries into action.

On occasion a lesson is followed by a ✎ **Digging Deeper** section, which gives you additional information and resources to probe further into some issues raised in that lesson.

There are many ways to use this guide—in personal devotions, group studies, discussions with friends and family, and Sunday school classes. And, of course, it's an ideal study aid when you're listening to its corresponding *Insight for Living* radio series.

To benefit most from this study guide, we would encourage you to consider it a spiritual journal. That's why we've included space in the **Living Insights** for recording your thoughts and discoveries. We hope you'll return to those sections often for review and encouragement as you continue to grow in your walk with Christ.

Ken Gire

Ken Gire
Coauthor of Text

Bryce Klabunde

Bryce Klabunde
Coauthor of Text
Author of Living Insights

A STUDY OF PHILEMON, 2 JOHN, 3 JOHN, AND JUDE

NEW
TESTAMENT
POSTCARDS

Chapter 1

A POSTCARD TO PHILEMON
Philemon

O f the thirteen letters Paul wrote in the New Testament, Philemon is the shortest—only twenty-five verses. It's like a postcard, really, but don't let the length deceive you. Though short in size, it's long in truth.

Writing from Rome, Paul addresses a slave owner named Philemon. Paul's purpose isn't to confront a heresy or straighten out a doctrinal confusion. Instead, with the personal tone of an intercessory prayer, he writes to restore a broken relationship. He appeals to Philemon to welcome back Onesimus, a runaway slave who has become a Christian through Paul's ministry.

Between the lines of this picture postcard of forgiveness is a message for us all—a message about second chances and showing mercy. A message about equality in Christ and the power of the gospel to transcend social boundaries. A message about grace.

The Historical Background

As with any correspondence, Paul's postcard to Philemon bears the imprint of the context in which it was written.

Flight to Freedom

At the time, Paul was living in Rome under house arrest, awaiting a trial before Caesar. Though in chains, he was free to proclaim Christ to all who came to him (Acts 28:16–31). As he later told the Philippian believers, his confinement actually "turned out for the greater progress of the gospel" (Phil. 1:12). He was able to reach people he might never have reached otherwise, including the soldiers who guarded him . . . and a certain young slave named Onesimus.

Onesimus was one of about sixty million slaves who shouldered the weight of the Roman Empire. Auctioned off like animals, slaves were destined to a life of backbreaking labor and degrading treatment. In the early days of the empire, Roman law offered them little protection from their master's whip. Commentator William Barclay describes some of the inhumanities they endured.

> A slave was not a person; he was a living tool. A master had absolute power over his slaves. "He can box their ears or condemn them to hard labour—making them, for instance, work in chains upon his lands in the country, or in a sort of prison-factory. Or, he may punish them with blows of the rod, the lash or the knot; he can brand them upon the forehead, if they are thieves or runaways, or, in the end, if they prove irreclaimable, he can crucify them."[1]

As a fugitive slave, Onesimus was in constant danger of being found out. His only hope for survival was to flee to Rome and lose himself in the faceless sea of people.

Finding the Ultimate Freedom

Before he ran away from Philemon, Onesimus appears to have stolen something from his master, possibly to finance his flight (Philem. 18). So not only was he a fugitive, he was a thief—a candidate for branding, or worse, if he was caught and returned. Freedom would not have felt too free with thoughts like that binding his every move.

Fortunately for him, God had a freedom waiting in the wings that was higher and wider than anything he had ever dreamed of.

Somehow, the Lord brought Onesimus into contact with Paul, who introduced him to the Savior. Onesimus reached out in faith, and at once his shackles of fear and shame dropped to the ground. In Christ, the fugitive found forgiveness. Now he was *really* free.

Liberty in Christ, however, doesn't mean being absolved from all earthly debts and responsibilities. He had been made righteous in Christ's eyes, but Paul knew that Onesimus now needed to make things right with Philemon. Returning to his master, however, meant dealing with two risky issues.

• First, there was the matter of property loss. When Onesimus

---

1. William Barclay, *The Letters to Timothy, Titus, and Philemon*, rev. ed., The Daily Study Bible series (Philadelphia, Pa.: Westminster Press, 1975), p. 270.

ran away, he cost Philemon the amount of the item he had stolen as well as the price his master had originally paid for him. So Onesimus left behind not only a fractured relationship but an unresolved debt.

- Second, there was the matter of an angry master. Christ had forgiven Onesimus . . . but would Philemon? Could the Christian master accept the repentant slave as a brother in the faith? It was the ultimate test of Christian fellowship and the power of the gospel to break down social walls.

With these two issues on the table, Paul sat down to write Philemon a note for Onesimus himself to hand deliver.

The Contents of Paul's Postcard

As we look at the text of Paul's postcard, four divisions emerge: a greeting, a commendation, a request, and a promise.

Greeting

Paul begins his note with a humble and affectionate salutation.

> Paul, a prisoner of Christ Jesus, and Timothy our brother, to Philemon our beloved brother and fellow worker, and to Apphia our sister, and to Archippus our fellow soldier, and to the church in your house: Grace to you and peace from God our Father and the Lord Jesus Christ. (vv. 1–3)

Unpretentiously, Paul refers to himself as "a prisoner of Christ Jesus" rather than an "apostle."[2] He owes his life to Christ, as does Philemon—who was apparently one of Paul's converts living in Colossae.[3] Owning a home spacious enough to house the church and owning at least one slave, Philemon was probably a man of some means. Apphia (possibly his wife) and Archippus (possibly his son) shared in the ministry.

---

2. See the first verse in Romans; 1 and 2 Corinthians; Galatians; Ephesians; Colossians; 1 and 2 Timothy; and Titus.

3. "He appears to have been a resident of Colossae, since his slave Onesimus is described in the Colossian letter as 'one of you' (4:9)." Curtis Vaughan, *Colossians and Philemon*, the Bible Study Commentary series (Grand Rapids, Mich.: Zondervan Publishing House, Lamplighter Books, 1980), p. 123.

Paul asks God to show "grace" and "peace" to Philemon. Both words strengthen his plea. As Paul appeals to God to show grace and peace to Philemon, so he will ask his friend to show a spirit of grace and peace to Onesimus.

Commendation

Before he lays out his request, Paul expresses his gratitude for Philemon.

> I thank my God always, making mention of you in my prayers, because I hear of your love, and of the faith which you have toward the Lord Jesus, and toward all the saints; and I pray that the fellowship of your faith may become effective through the knowledge of every good thing which is in you for Christ's sake. For I have come to have much joy and comfort in your love, because the hearts of the saints have been refreshed through you, brother. (vv. 4–7)

An expert craftsman of letters, Paul builds a base of good rapport with Philemon before raising the delicate subject of Onesimus. He wastes not one word on flattery. His purpose is to encourage his brother in Christ and, at the same time, call him to a high moral standard—a standard Philemon has already been displaying in his refreshing spirit of love.

Request

Without pulling rank or issuing orders, Paul now appeals to Philemon on the basis of love:

> Therefore, though I have enough confidence in Christ to order you to do that which is proper, yet for love's sake I rather appeal to you—since I am such a person as Paul, the aged, and now also a prisoner of Christ Jesus—I appeal to you for my child, whom I have begotten in my imprisonment, Onesimus. (vv. 8–10)

Onesimus—a name that grates over Philemon's tongue and leaves the bitter aftertaste of disloyalty and desertion. Paul mentions it here for the first time, wisely sweetening the word with the phrase, "my child, whom I have begotten in my imprisonment."

In verse 11, Paul explains the radical change in Onesimus' life as a result of his new birth in Christ:

> Who formerly was useless to you, but now is useful both to you and to me.

The one picture Philemon had in his mind was of the *useless* Onesimus of the past—a runaway and a thief. A more recent photo, however, which Paul reveals in the following verses, shows a *useful* Onesimus—a minister and a brother.

> And I have sent him back to you in person, that is, sending my very heart, whom I wished to keep with me, that in your behalf he might minister to me in my imprisonment for the gospel; but without your consent I did not want to do anything, that your goodness should not be as it were by compulsion, but of your own free will. For perhaps he was for this reason parted from you for a while, that you should have him back forever, no longer as a slave, but more than a slave, a beloved brother, especially to me, but how much more to you, both in the flesh and in the Lord. If then you regard me a partner, accept him as you would me. (vv. 12–17)

Paul's appeal is based on an advocacy clause in Roman law. Runaway slaves could return to their masters and be protected if they first went to their master's friend and secured support for their cause. The friend became an advocate, or mediator, who appealed to the slave's owner for grace and understanding. There were even some instances where the master not only accepted the slave back but adopted the slave into his family.[4]

Paul hoped Philemon would accept Onesimus with the open arms of a brother, not only in the spiritual sense—"in the Lord"—but in the physical sense as well—"in the flesh" (v. 16).

Promise

Nobody asked for fewer favors than Paul did. But now he asks for one, not so much for his sake, but for Onesimus' and Christ's

---

4. See J. Sidlow Baxter, "The Pastoral Epistles," in *Explore the Book*, one-volume ed. (Grand Rapids, Mich.: Zondervan Publishing House, Academie Books, 1966), pp. 253–254.

and the church's sake. Paul even goes so far as to offer his own wallet on behalf of Onesimus:

> But if he has wronged you in any way, or owes you anything, charge that to my account; I, Paul, am writing this with my own hand, I will repay it (lest I should mention to you that you owe to me even your own self as well). Yes, brother, let me benefit from you in the Lord; refresh my heart in Christ. (vv. 18–20)

Paul uses a subtle play on words in verse 20. *Benefit* in Greek is related to the root of Onesimus' name, which means "profitable." Paul is saying, "I am sending Onesimus to you, my friend, all debts paid. Now let me in return, receive from you a touch of *onesimus* through your willingness to forgive him."

Then, in verses 21–24, Paul signs off with a word of confidence that Philemon will do the right thing, and he sends his greetings to a few other believers in Colossae. As a postscript, he lovingly leaves Philemon with this prayer:

> The grace of the Lord Jesus Christ be with your spirit. (v. 25)

What was Philemon's response to this brief letter? Did he forgive Onesimus? In thumbing through the New Testament mail, we might expect to find a quick telegram from Philemon with his reply, but it is nowhere to be found. However, a church father named Ignatius, writing fifty years later in a letter to the Ephesians, addressed their wonderful minister, their bishop, named Onesimus. In this letter, according to William Barclay,

> Ignatius makes exactly the same pun as Paul made —he is Onesimus by name and Onesimus by nature, the profitable one to Christ. It may well be that the runaway slave had become with the passing years the great bishop of Ephesus.[5]

If this is true, Bishop Onesimus of Ephesus may have played a large role in including his story in the New Testament canon. It could be that he wanted the world to know how a useless runaway became useful through the transforming power of the Cross.

---

5. Barclay, *Timothy, Titus, and Philemon*, p. 275.

Application

This ancient postcard to Philemon has a present-day postmark, with our names on the forwarding address. Let's look at some of the ways it applies to us.

Every Christian was once a fugitive. Enslaved to sin through Adam's fall, we ran from God, following our own paths instead of His. As Isaiah wrote, "All of us like sheep have gone astray, Each of us has turned to his own way" (Isa. 53:6).

Our guilt was great and our penalty was severe. Like Onesimus, we lived in fear of being found out. Guilt tormented our souls, and no matter where we ran, the grim sentence of death hung over our heads.

Grace allowed us the right of appeal. Pleading our case was our Advocate, Jesus Christ, who stood before the Judge and mediated on our behalf (1 Tim. 2:5).

Christ said, "Charge that to My account!" With His blood, He paid the debt we owe the Father for our sins (Col. 2:13–14). We are set free!

As a result, our Master has accepted us back and adopted us into His family. Arms opened wide, the Father welcomes us into His loving embrace.

> But when the fulness of the time came, God sent forth His Son, born of a woman, born under the Law, in order that He might redeem those who were under the Law, that we might receive the adoption as sons. And because you are sons, God has sent forth the Spirit of His Son into our hearts, crying, "Abba! Father!" *Therefore you are no longer a slave, but a son;* and if a son, then an heir through God. (Gal. 4:4–7, emphasis added)

Living Insights

Every day, another runaway tries to throw off the shackles of an intolerable life and make a dash for freedom. The alcoholic drinks until all pain is left far behind. The adulterous spouse runs from a dying marriage into a lover's waiting arms. The depressed executive slams the door of communication and flees to a world of privacy and silence.

If you've sensed a family member, friend, or even yourself running from relationships and responsibilities, the story of Onesimus is for you.

His experience demonstrates that running away may relieve the pressure for a while, but it doesn't solve the problem. The green grass looks so inviting from the other side. But those who've hopped the fence of an affair or a divorce know how quickly it withers in the blistering wind of reality.

Once we've made our escape, we think that the Lord won't want us back. But that's not true. Onesimus also teaches us that with Christ's help, a repentant runaway can always return home. The Lord is always willing to forgive (Ps. 86:5). He can even help us mend the fences we trampled on our flight to freedom.

If you've been running, are you ready to go home? What's your first step?

_____

_____

_____

If you have a runaway loved one, how can you tear down the walls on your side to make him or her want to come back?

_____

_____

_____

Christ forgives the runaway, but are we willing to forgive ourselves and those who hurt us? Can we open our arms to His grace? It's the only way home.

 ## Digging Deeper

Considering the abuses of slavery and its destruction of human dignity, why didn't Paul denounce it in his letter to Philemon? There's not one simple answer to that question, for it touches on the delicate balance between our duty to submit to existing powers (Matt. 17:24–27; Rom. 13:1–7; 1 Tim. 2:1–4) and our duty to influence society as salt and light (Matt. 5:13–16). For further study on this complex and crucial subject, we recommend the following sources:

Colson, Charles, with Ellen Santilli Vaughn. *Kingdoms in Conflict.* New York, N.Y.: William Morrow; Grand Rapids, Mich.: Zondervan Publishing House, 1987.

Davis, David Brion. *The Problem of Slavery in Western Culture.* Ithaca, N.Y.: Cornell University Press, 1966, pp. 29–106.

Drake, Thomas E. *Quakers and Slavery in America.* New Haven, Conn.: Yale University Press, 1950.

Scherer, Lester B. *Slavery and the Churches in Early America 1619–1819.* Grand Rapids, Mich.: William B. Eerdmans Publishing Co., 1975.

Stott, John. *Involvement, Volume 1: Being a Responsible Christian in a Non-Christian Society.* A Crucial Questions Book. Old Tappan, N.J.: Fleming H. Revell Co., 1985.

Westerman, William L. *The Slave Systems of Greek and Roman Antiquity.* Philadelphia, Pa.: American Philosophical Society, 1955.

Chapter 2

A POSTCARD TO A LADY
AND HER KIDS

2 John

From its headwaters in northern Minnesota, the Mississippi River meanders southward to the Gulf of Mexico, spawning and sustaining life along its nearly 2,400-mile journey. To those who know it well, the river is a gentle giant, an untiring bestower of good gifts. It is a bountiful, self-replenishing storehouse of nutrients for farmland. It is a refreshing aviary for birds. A busy highway for barges.

However, let it leave its boundaries, and this gentle giant becomes an unwieldy beast.

More than forty dams and about 1,600 miles of levees attempt to control the mighty tide, but there are frightening times when the river puffs up its chest and pushes over these meager defenses. The floods of 1993 testify to the widespread damage the river can cause: prime bottomland became lakes, entire towns were destroyed, and levees in eight states were wiped out.[1]

In many ways, love is like the Mississippi River. It flows with life-giving power, but without control, without boundaries, it can do great harm. In the name of loving sinners, we can go too far, to the point that we tolerate, accept, and even justify sin. This kind of love calmly sets others adrift in dangerous waters rather than moving them from death to life.

The little postcard of 2 John shows us how to keep love within safe boundaries by building in our lives two solid river banks—truth and discernment.

Introductory Questions

Only thirteen verses, 2 John barely fills a single sheet of papyrus. It's like a note we might write and drop in the mail to a close friend. As a personal letter, it cradles some secrets we as outsiders aren't

---

1. *The Concise Columbia Encyclopedia* (New York, N.Y.: Columbia University Press, 1991), see "Mississippi." From Microsoft Bookshelf © 1987–1994 Microsoft Corporation. All rights reserved. And "Mississippi (river)," Microsoft ® Encarta. Copyright © 1993 Microsoft Corporation. Copyright © 1993 Funk & Wagnall's Corporation.

privy to. The opening is cloaked in mystery: "The elder to the chosen lady and her children." Who is the elder? Who is the lady? What's the situation? These are some questions we should try to answer before reading any further.

Who Is "the Elder"?

The Greek term for elder is *presbuteros*, which generally means "old man." It can also designate a religious rank or office. Although no names appear in the letter, we can feel certain that the author is the apostle John, who was living in exile on the island of Patmos. The fingerprints of his language and style indelibly mark this letter, which is why he didn't have to sign his name—the people knew he was the author.[2] As a modern clergyman might sign a letter to his congregation simply, "Your Pastor," the omission of John's name actually lends intimacy and warmth to his letter.

Who Is "the Chosen Lady"?

Some commentators view "the chosen lady" as the church personified, and "her children" as the members.[3] However, John's consistent personal references ("lady," v. 5; her "house," v. 10; and her "sister," v. 13) lead us to believe that he's writing to a literal woman. Like Lydia in the book of Acts (see 16:14–15, 40), this lady of 2 John was a gracious hostess, opening her home for the sake of the ministry. Her river of love flowed freely to anyone who knocked on her door, including the traveling teachers and prophets who came to town.

What's the Situation?

Because the New Testament was not yet a complete, written book, early Christians depended on itinerant prophets and teachers to supply the divine revelation they needed to build their faith. They welcomed these traveling preachers, often housing and feeding them in the finest style they could afford. Unfortunately, not all of the roving reverends were worthy of such warm hospitality. It was not uncommon for wicked men to exploit the trusting Christians.

2. Also, this note possibly came in a bundle of letters addressed to the church, making a more specific greeting unnecessary. And perhaps John wanted to protect himself and his readers from persecution should the letter fall into the wrong hands.

3. See J. R. W. Stott, *The Epistles of John* (1964; reprint, Grand Rapids, Mich.: William B. Eerdmans Publishing Co., 1969), pp. 200–2.

Even the secular writers attested to their abuses:

> Lucian, the Greek writer, in his work called the *Peregrinus*, draws the picture of a man who had found the easiest possible way of making a living without working. He was an itinerant charlatan who lived on the fat of the land by travelling round the various communities of the Christians, settling down wherever he liked and living luxuriously at their expense.[4]

The problem became so widespread that strict rules were eventually laid down in *The Didache*, or "The Teaching," an early book of church order. The following excerpt illustrates the kind of precautions that had to be taken.

> Let every apostle that cometh unto you be received as the Lord. And he shall stay one day, and, if need be, the next also, but, if he stay three, he is a false prophet. And, when the apostle goeth forth, let him take nothing save bread, till he reach his lodging, but, if he ask money, he is a false prophet. . . . But not everyone that speaketh in the Spirit is a prophet, but if he has the manners of the Lord. By their manners, therefore, shall the prophet and the false prophet be known. And no prophet who ordereth a table in the Spirit shall eat of it, else he is a false prophet. And every prophet that teacheth the truth, if he doeth not what he teacheth, is a false prophet. . . . Whosoever shall say in the Spirit: Give me money, or any other thing, ye shall not hearken to him: but, if he bid you give for others who are in need, let no man judge him.
>
> Let everyone that cometh in the name of the Lord be received. . . . If he be minded to settle among you, and be a craftsman, let him work and eat. But, if he hath no trade, according to your understanding, provide that he shall not live idle among you, being a Christian. But, if he will not do this, he is a Christmonger: of such men beware.[5]

4. William Barclay, *The Letters of John and Jude*, rev. ed., The Daily Study Bible series (Philadelphia, Pa.: Westminster Press, 1976), pp. 133–34.

5. As quoted by Barclay, *The Letters of John and Jude*, p. 134.

John caught wind of some of these foul-smelling "Christmongers" swarming around this woman's home. Naively, she was taking them in, not realizing that they were spoiling the church. While affirming her charitable spirit, John sends her an urgent message: *Make sure your love has limits.*

Expository Investigation

Not wanting to discourage his friend, John wrapped his words in velvet. Undoubtedly, his kind introduction brought a smile to her face.

Introduction

> The elder to the chosen lady and her children, whom I love in truth; and not only I, but also all who know the truth, for the sake of the truth which abides in us and will be with us forever. (2 John 1–2)

His love for this lady and her children is embanked "in truth." It is proper. It is pure. He is writing "for the sake of the truth," because when this levee crumbles, love gets out of hand. Notice, in verse 3, how inseparably he links truth and love—two everlasting, ever-balanced principles:

> Grace, mercy and peace will be with us, from God the Father and from Jesus Christ, the Son of the Father, in truth and love. (v. 3)

The lady understands the importance of these principles, for, as John notes with a word of praise, she has reared her children in them:

> I was very glad to find some of your children walking in truth, just as we have received commandment to do from the Father. (v. 4)

The whole tone of John's letter embodies the very teaching he is trying to convey. In the introduction, he lovingly greets her, and in the next section, his voice does not fade as he exhorts her in the truth.

Exhortation

> And now I ask you, lady, not as writing to you a new commandment, but the one which we have had from the beginning, that we love one another. And this is love, that we walk according to His commandments. This is the commandment, just as you have heard from

the beginning, that you should walk in it. (vv. 5–6)

Christ commanded us to love one another (John 13:34), but He never meant for us to do so blindly. If we give our affections to a person, and he or she drags us away from the truth, that's not Christian love. "*This* is love," John says, "that we walk according to His commandments." The test of love is whether it leads us closer to Christ. True love never compromises its standards. Never consents to sin. And never, *never* embraces evil.

Instruction

Love is the hinge on which hospitality turns to open its door. But just as a door has hinges, it also has a lock. And love never opens the door to a wolf—even if it's dressed in sheep's clothing. This is the thrust of John's instruction:

> For many deceivers have gone out into the world, those who do not acknowledge Jesus Christ as coming in the flesh. This is the deceiver and the anti-christ. Watch yourselves, that you might not lose what we have accomplished, but that you may receive a full reward. Anyone who goes too far and does not abide in the teaching of Christ, does not have God; the one who abides in the teaching, he has both the Father and the Son. (2 John 7–9)

The false prophets may have pulled the wool over the lady's eyes, but, in verse 7, John removes the impostors' white fleece to reveal their true identity. Although they speak kindly about Christ, they are really against Him and His teaching—"anti-Christ." In this case, they denied that He came in the flesh, which was part of the Gnostic heresy that blighted the early church.[6]

By opening her floodgates of love to these false teachers, the lady was, in fact, aiding and abetting the enemy. This is why John says,

> If anyone comes to you and does not bring this teaching, do not receive him into your house, and

6. Basing their teaching on the Greek philosophy of dualism, the Gnostics viewed the spirit as good and matter as evil. They believed that Christ could not have come in the flesh, otherwise He would have been tainted with evil. Instead, they argued that Christ only appeared to take on human form. For more information on Gnosticism, see Peter Jones' *The Gnostic Empire Strikes Back: An Old Heresy for the New Age* (Phillipsburg, N.J.: Presbyterian and Reformed Publishing Co., 1992).

do not give him a greeting; for the one who gives him a greeting participates in his evil deeds. (vv. 10–11)

The world is full of deceivers, people who would lure us away from the truth and our eternal reward. And no area is so crowded with them as the borders of religion. Most false teachers use the Bible as their base but either add to or take away from its true meaning. The following fundamentals of our faith form a good checklist with which we can test the teachers who knock on our doors or come into our homes through the TV, radio, print, or computer.

- Inerrancy of Scripture (2 Tim. 3:16; 2 Pet. 1:21)

- Virgin birth and deity of Christ (Isa. 7:14; Matt. 1:18–25; Luke 1:26–38; John 1:1, 14; 8:53–58; Col. 1:15–20; Heb. 1:3, 8)

- Sinless nature and life of Christ (Heb. 4:15)

- Substitutionary death of the Savior (Rom. 5:6–8; 2 Cor. 5:21)

- Effectiveness of Christ's blood to cleanse sin (Heb. 9:22, 26; 1 John 1:7, 9)

- Bodily resurrection of Christ (Luke 24:36–43; 1 Cor. 15:1–11)

- Ascension of Christ and His present ministry to the believer (Acts 1:6–9; John 14:12–21; Rom. 8:34; Eph. 4:7–10)

- Literal, future return of Christ to the earth (John 14:1–3; 1 Thess. 4:13–18)

Conclusion

These truths provide the necessary boundaries for our love, without building a dam to stop it up. In fact, John enhances the flow of that love with a final word about joy—the result of keeping love and truth in balance.

Having many things to write to you, I do not want to do so with paper and ink; but I hope to come to you and speak face to face, that your joy may be made full. (2 John 12)

Application

You can keep John's postcard handy by remembering these principles. First, *love coexists with the truth.* As commentator John R. W.

Stott states so well, "Our love grows soft if it is not strengthened by truth, and our truth grows hard if it is not softened by love."[7]

Second, *discrimination and discernment are essential to life and happiness*. John isn't saying we should slam the door in the face of those who believe differently from us. His point is this: Be discerning about who you invite into your life. Be courageous and stand for what you believe. Confronting error with truth may be difficult, but, in the long run, it is the most loving thing to do.

Living Insights

The best way to guard against error is to know the truth. Do you need to shore up your bank of truth? Take a few moments to look up the verses in our list of fundamentals on page 15. Based on what you find, briefly explain in your own words what each doctrine means.

Inerrancy: _____

_____

Virgin birth/deity of Christ: _____

_____

Christ's sinless life and nature: _____

_____

Substitutionary death of Christ: _____

_____

Power of Christ's blood to cleanse sin: _____

_____

Christ's bodily resurrection: _____

_____

---

7. Stott, *The Epistles of John*, p. 205.

Ascension and present ministry of Christ: _____

_____

Christ's return: _____

_____

Do you know someone who denies any of these truths? Has this person caused you to question your beliefs? Do you sense that he or she is pulling you away from Christ?

Based on 2 John 10–11, what levee do you need to build in your relationship with this person?

_____

_____

What encouragement does Paul give you in Ephesians 4:14–15?

_____

_____

What words of truth do you need to speak to this person?

_____

_____

"Speaking the truth in love" isn't easy. But it's the best thing you could do for them . . . and for yourself.

Chapter 3

A POSTCARD OF CANDID TRUTH

3 John

Postcards. Those glossy pictures of paradise printed on a four-by-six mailer. Ever notice that the scenes on postcards always look better than the actual place? The sun shines brighter, the surf curls rounder, the palm trees stretch taller. *This* is what you had in mind when you planned your vacation, not the overcrowded, billboarded reality you saw when you arrived.

Unlike the postcards in a tourist shop, the postcards in the New Testament don't airbrush the truth about the early church. There was the scorching heat of persecution, along with the flies and mosquitoes of heresy that needed constant swatting. And, like sand in your bathing suit, there were always abrasive believers who rubbed you the wrong way. The first-century church was not the Edenic garden spot we like to imagine.

As we turn to the postcard of 3 John, we see a genuine scene from the New Testament church. No glossy coating. No special tinting. Filling the entire frame is reality, the good and the bad together in one picture.

Comparison of 2 John to 3 John

It's helpful to view 3 John in the light of 2 John. By placing the two postcards side by side, we can observe several illuminating contrasts.

2 John	3 John
Written to a lady and her children	Written to a man and his acquaintances
Problem: a lady is receiving the wrong kind of travelers	*Problem:* a man is rejecting the right kind of travelers
A matter of misplaced hospitality	A matter of missing hospitality
Needed: truth to balance love	*Needed:* love to balance truth

18

No names are mentioned in 2 John, except for the Lord's, while three names appear in 3 John: Gaius,[1] Diotrephes, and Demetrius. From John's brief and intriguing message to these men, we can piece together the story between the lines.

Analysis of 3 John

The three names form a natural outline for 3 John: Gaius is the recipient of *encouragement* (vv. 1–8); Diotrephes is the subject of *criticism* (vv. 9–11); Demetrius is an example of a good *testimony* (v. 12).

Encouragement of Gaius

John colors his picture of Gaius in warm and affectionate hues:

> The elder to the beloved Gaius, whom I love in truth.
> Beloved, I pray that in all respects you may prosper and be in good health, just as your soul prospers. (vv. 1–2)

Four times John calls Gaius "beloved"—twice here and twice later (see vv. 5, 11). He loves him "in truth," that is, in the truth of Christ, who unites all believers in Himself.

John prays that his friend will prosper physically just as he is prospering spiritually.[2] Perhaps his prayer is a response to reports that Gaius is in poor health. In spite of his afflictions (or perhaps *because* of them—see Ps. 119:71), Gaius' devotion to Christ has flourished.

We hear a lot about prosperity, that insatiable American dream of ageless beauty and boundless wealth. But who is preaching a prosperity of the soul? Who is pursuing that dream? What does it look like? In verses 3–4, John points it out in Gaius:

---

1. Gaius was a common name in the Roman empire, like John or Jim today. Three other men in the New Testament bore this name: Gaius the Macedonian, who was with Paul at the riot of Ephesus (Acts 19:29); Gaius of Derbe, who transported a collection from his church to the suffering Christians in Jerusalem (20:4); and Gaius of Corinth, who was baptized by Paul and who served as Paul's host (1 Cor. 1:14; Rom. 16:23). Could one of these men be the Gaius in 3 John? Probably not. This Gaius was John's convert (3 John 3–4) and bears nothing in common with the others.

2. The Gnostics looked down on material things, viewing them as trivial at best, evil at worst. John's interest in Gaius' material and physical health reflects the Lord's concern for our whole being. He's not just a God of the soul; He's a God of the body as well.

> For I was very glad when brethren came and bore
> witness to your truth, that is, how you are walking
> in truth. I have no greater joy than this, to hear of
> my children walking in the truth. (vv. 3–4)

Just as a parent delights in a child's first step, John bursts a button when he hears that Gaius, his spiritual son, has not only taken that first step of faith but continues "walking in truth." We can see how he put shoe leather on the truth in verses 5–8.

> Beloved, you are acting faithfully in whatever
> you accomplish for the brethren, and especially
> when they are strangers; and they bear witness to
> your love before the church; and you will do well
> to send them on their way in a manner worthy of
> God. For they went out for the sake of the Name,
> accepting nothing from the Gentiles. Therefore we
> ought to support such men, that we may be fellow
> workers with the truth. (vv. 5–8)

Gaius demonstrated Christ's love when he welcomed a group of traveling ministers into his home. Who were these preachers? Why did they come to Gaius' church? To answer these questions, we need to go back to New Testament days.

In the first century, there were two types of ministers—the "pioneers" and the "settlers." The pioneers were apostles, prophets, and evangelists who helped people come to faith in Christ, developed a nucleus of a new church, and then moved on to follow the frontier. The settlers were local pastors, teachers, and elders who remained in their areas permanently, maturing their flocks. These established churches became the primary base of support for the itinerant pioneers (see 1 Cor. 9:1–14).

At first, the baby churches eagerly welcomed the wise teaching of the pioneers. But, as time passed, the church's wobbly legs grew stronger. They entered an awkward period of transition from dependence to independence, in which they still needed guidance but resented outside authority. A dangerous rift formed between the two groups, as tremors of resentment and refusals to offer hospitality radiated from the local church's leadership.

Gaius, in contrast, kept his doors open to these dedicated pioneers. And John encourages him to continue in this good work. Why? Because, first, these pioneers minister for the sake of Christ, not themselves. As emissaries for the King, they should be supported in "a manner worthy of God" (3 John 6). Second, they work without any compensation from the world (v. 7) and would starve without the church's help. And third, to support them in their efforts is to be "fellow workers with the truth" (v. 8).

Not everyone was as hospitable as Gaius, however; and John now shifts his focus to a particularly rancorous church leader named Diotrephes.

Criticism of Diotrephes

John's sketch of this man is darkly smudged with charcoaled lines that accentuate his harsh character.

> I wrote something to the church; but Diotrephes, who loves to be first among them, does not accept what we say. For this reason, if I come, I will call attention to his deeds which he does, unjustly accusing us with wicked words; and not satisfied with this, neither does he himself receive the brethren, and he forbids those who desire to do so, and puts them out of the church. Beloved, do not imitate what is evil, but what is good. The one who does good is of God; the one who does evil has not seen God. (vv. 9–11)

Viciously guarding "his turf," Diotrephes shook off John's teaching in a previous letter and assaulted the apostle with sharp-edged accusations. Intimidation shuddered through the church as he slammed the door in the faces of traveling prophets and teachers, forbade the members to welcome them, and expelled them from the church if they did.

What would cause a leader to become so jealous and defensive? In verse 9, John puts his finger on the core problem: Diotrephes "loves to be first." That little microchip description stores a world of information about his character. He runs on a me-first, look-out-for-number-one program. Type any set of variables into the computer, and the program quickly processes an automatic response. You know immediately what his relationships are like. *He's* going to be the one served, not the one serving. Like the scribes and Pharisees, who "love the place of honor at banquets" (Matt. 23:6), you can bet he'll be the one pushing to get the best seat—not the one washing anybody's feet.

An outbreak of "Diotrephes' disease" can spread rapidly through a church. As strong-minded people move into positions of influence, they begin intimidating others—practically hypnotizing them. The problem usually isn't a matter of theology as much as pride. Before long, the self-willed, stubborn leaders have bred a whole congregation of self-willed, stubborn followers. The doors of ministry close, and the body dies. It's a sad fate for any church. That's why John pleads with Gaius to resist the disease: "Do not imitate what is evil, but what is good" (3 John 11).

John gives Gaius an opportunity to do what is right by receiving Demetrius, a good man who deserves a warm welcome.

Testimony of Demetrius

From the dark portrait of Diotrephes, John turns his attention to the delightful picture of Demetrius:

> Demetrius has received a good testimony from everyone, and from the truth itself; and we also bear witness, and you know that our witness is true. (v. 12)

Demetrius was probably John's emissary, passing on his instructions and delivering this short letter. It was critical for John to keep the lines of communication open between himself and the church. So he sent his best man, Demetrius, with three impressive references. First, everyone Demetrius knew vouched for him; second, his life lined up with the truth, which testified on his behalf; and third, John gave him his personal stamp of approval.

Concluding Observations

John's realistic postcard shows us that the early church was certainly not free from conflict. New Testament churches had the same kinds of problems our churches have today. However, despite their conflicts, the ministries went on. God used these cracked, failure-prone vessels to feed a spiritually starving world (see 2 Cor. 4:7).

In the final verses of his letter, John affirms his confidence in the church. Instead of writing it off as a lost cause, he expresses a deep desire to visit Gaius. Until he arrives, he prays for God's peace to settle on the church.

> I had many things to write to you, but I am not willing to write them to you with pen and ink; but I hope to see you shortly, and we shall speak face to

face. Peace be to you. The friends greet you. Greet
the friends by name. (3 John 13–14)

Relevance of the Postcard

Every church has its Diotrephes, who will try to cast a gray
shadow across the ministry—unjustly accusing leaders, shutting out
people in need, intimidating church members. Emerging from the
cloud is a Gaius or a Demetrius, who display a rainbow of virtues—
hospitality, generosity, integrity, and purity. Follow these leaders,
because they bear the marks of those who walk in truth.

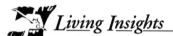 *Living Insights*

Diotrephes' pride took over his life in stages. The first stage was
resistance: he refused to submit to authority by not accepting John's
teaching (3 John 9). Second was *criticism*: he started hurling unjust
accusations at those in authority (v. 10a). Third was *isolation*: he
shut himself off from outside instruction and correction—he didn't
"receive the brethren" (v. 10b). Fourth was *control*: he forbade the
people from listening to any teaching except his own (v. 10c).

Maybe you've seen others follow this downward path; perhaps
you're in one of the stages now. Shine the following questions into
your heart. What signs of pride do you see?

Am I resisting authority in my life?

_____

_____

_____

Do I have a critical spirit?

_____

_____

_____

Have I isolated myself from people who might instruct or correct me?

_____

_____

_____

Am I controlling people with intimidation or threats?

_____

_____

_____

What warnings do the following Proverbs shout to you about the dangers of pride?

Proverbs 11:2 _____

_____

Proverbs 13:10 _____

_____

Proverbs 16:5, 18 _____

_____

Proverbs 29:1 _____

_____

Jesus prescribes a cure for "Diotrephes' disease" in His teaching against the Pharisees and scribes. According to Matthew 23:1–12, what are His instructions?

_____

_____

_____

How can you put Christ's remedy into action?

_____

_____

_____

Chapter 4

THE ACTS OF THE APOSTATES
Jude 1–4

W ho of us hasn't at one time complained, "Doctrine is too dull. I need practical answers for my real-life problems"? So we search out "experts" who can tell us how to be a better parent, how to juggle career and family, how to navigate life's emotional rapids. In our quest to soothe our soul's outcry, however, we sometimes cut loose our doctrinal anchors, setting ourselves adrift in a confusing sea of prepackaged self-help books each promising happiness in its own way.

Yes, we need help and answers; there's no doubt about that. The trouble comes, though, when we choose popular opinions over lasting orthodoxy, emotional comfort over scriptural credibility, ten easy steps over truth.

Such an individualized, "personal happiness at any cost" atmosphere fosters an environment ripe for apostasy. Jesus warned that the end times would be marked by a wholesale falling away from the truth.

> "At that time many will fall away . . . and many false prophets will arise, and will mislead many." (Matt. 24:10–11)

And Paul echoed Jesus' alarm:

> Let no one in any way deceive you, for [the day of the Lord] will not come unless the apostasy comes first. (2 Thess. 2:3a)

> But the Spirit explicitly says that in later times some will fall away from the faith. (1 Tim. 4:1a)

> For the time will come when they will not endure sound doctrine; but wanting to have their ears tickled, they will accumulate for themselves teachers in accordance to their own desires; and will turn away their ears from the truth, and will turn aside to myths. (2 Tim. 4:3–4)

Sounds like our times, doesn't it? How can we stand strong in our beliefs and guard ourselves against those who would undermine the truth of our faith? Answering that question is what the postcard of Jude is all about.

The Author and the Audience

Jude begins his message by introducing himself and his audience:

> Jude, a bond-servant of Jesus Christ, and brother of James, to those who are the called, beloved in God the Father, and kept for Jesus Christ: May mercy and peace and love be multiplied to you. (Jude 1–2)

Jude's brother was the same man who wrote the book James. Both of them were Jesus' half-brothers (Mary was their mother, but Jesus had a heavenly Father). Jude, who at one time thought his oldest brother had lost His senses (see Mark 3:21), now described himself as His "bond-servant" (Jude 1). His singular goal in life was to be forever at Jesus' disposal.

In this letter Jude addressed his thoughts to those who are "called," "beloved," and "kept"—called by the Spirit, loved by God the Father, and kept safe by Christ.[1] We could fill in our names here, for Jude's words of warning are not addressed to one specific church or person but apply to Christians in every generation.[2]

The Admonition

Verse 3 expresses the heart of Jude's admonition:

> Beloved, while I was making every effort to write you about our common salvation, I felt the necessity to write to you appealing that you contend earnestly for the faith which was once for all delivered to the saints.

Jude had wanted to extol the wonders of the salvation he shared in common with his readers, but a more pressing need arose that

---

1. See Edward C. Pentecost, "Jude," in *The Bible Knowledge Commentary*, New Testament edition, ed. John F. Walvoord and Roy B. Zuck (Wheaton, Ill.: Scripture Press Publications, Victor Books, 1983), p. 919.

2. Pentecost further adds that "the tone of the letter demonstrates that the original recipients may have been Christian Jews of Palestine who were gathered into local fellowships. The references made to Old Testament incidents and to extrabiblical literature [vv. 5–11, 14–15] . . . all point to a people familiar with Old Testament history and possibly apocryphal literature." "Jude," p. 918.

abruptly caused him to switch subjects. If not dealt with now, this problem would derail the faith of his beloved readers.

What was the need that prompted Jude's theme? That the believers would "contend earnestly for the faith." The word for *contend* is a mouthful in Greek, *epagonizomai*. It means

> to struggle for, to contend for, to exercise great effort and exertion for something. The word was used of athletic contests and the struggle and effort of the athletes in their games.[3]

If you look at the word carefully, you'll see the root from which it's taken, *agonizomai*. We get our word *agonize* from it. The picture is of two formidable wrestlers grappling in an ancient, dirt-floored gymnasium. The air is thick and humid with the smell of sweat. Their muscles strain to the point of bursting as they "agonize" against each other for the prize of victory. That's the idea of *contend*.

Jude is saying, "Don't let anyone pin your faith to the ground without a struggle. It's worth fighting for, so don't be afraid to get in the dirt and wrestle for it."

So we're to contend earnestly—but for what exactly? What did Jude mean when he wrote of "the faith"? This "faith" has three clarifying facets to it.

1. This faith is the body of Christian doctrine found in the Scriptures in content and practice. It is more than our individual, personal salvation faith. It encompasses all that we believe about God, the Bible, sin, Christ, human nature, and so on.

2. The beliefs that make up the faith have been delivered "once for all" in the Scriptures. We can't change one word. They are our absolutes, our solid nucleus of truth that can't be amended, erased, or molded to suit each new generation's lifestyles.

3. God has delivered this faith not to a privileged few but to "the saints"—to every believer. Although His truth is a priceless treasure, He doesn't lock it under glass in a museum, kept only for the doctors of theology to touch. He wants us to handle it, to study it, to wear out its pages.

---

3. Fritz Rienecker, *A Linguistic Key to the Greek New Testament*, translated and edited by Cleon L. Rogers, Jr. (Grand Rapids, Mich.: Zondervan Publishing House, Regency Reference Library, 1980), p. 803.

Such generosity is risky, though, for some might mishandle and twist His precious Word—as indeed many have been doing since Jude's time.

The Apostates

Having urged his readers to fight for the faith, Jude now tells them why.

> For certain persons have crept in unnoticed, those who were long beforehand marked out for this condemnation, ungodly persons who turn the grace of our God into licentiousness and deny our only Master and Lord, Jesus Christ. (v. 4)

Another name for these "certain . . . ungodly persons" is *apostates*. These people didn't just drift away from God; they deliberately defected from Him. With defiance in their hearts, they purposefully opposed the mainstream teaching of the Christian faith and planted seeds of division and dissension in the believing community.

Unlike the apostles, however, who kept a high profile, the apostates "crept in unnoticed." The Greek word, *pareisduo*, has a sinister and secretive undertone to its meaning: "to get in by the side . . . to slip in by a side-door."[4] Barclay, in his commentary on Jude, vividly illustrates the term.

> It is used of the specious and seductive words of a clever pleader seeping gradually into the minds of a judge and jury; it is used of an outlaw slipping secretly back into the country from which he has been expelled; it is used of the slow and subtle entry of innovations into the life of state, which in the end undermine and break down the ancestral laws. It always indicates a stealthy insinuation of something evil into a society or situation.[5]

Like poison dropped furtively into someone's drink, these false teachers quietly penetrated the church. Their effect was lethal, poisoning the core of Christian truth in at least two ways.

4. Marvin R. Vincent, *Word Studies in the New Testament*, 2d ed. (McLean, Va.: MacDonald Publishing Co., 1888), vol. 1, p. 712.

5. William Barclay, *The Letters of John and Jude*, rev. ed., The Daily Study Bible series (Philadelphia, Pa.: Westminster Press, 1976), p. 179.

First, they "turn[ed] the grace of our God into licentiousness." Jude's word for *turn* means "to transpose."[6] They transposed grace from a major key to a minor key—from freedom to obey Christ to freedom to sin (compare Rom. 6:15–23). These false teachers viewed grace not as the way to life but as their ticket to guilt-free, unrestrained *licentiousness*. This word in Greek, *aselgeia*, represents the worst sort of perversion, as Barclay explains.

> Most men try to hide their sin; they have enough respect for common decency not to wish to be found out. But the *aselges* is the man who is so lost to decency that he does not care who sees his sin. It is not that he arrogantly and proudly flaunts it; it is simply that he can publicly do the most shameless things, because he has ceased to care for decency at all.[7]

Second, by their perversions, the apostates "den[ied] our only Master and Lord, Jesus Christ" (Jude 4). Exploitation of grace naturally leads to a denial of Christ's authority as Lord. For if grace supposedly sets us free to do as we please, we can choose to obey or not to obey Christ. In essence, apostate hearts say, "I'll take Christ . . . but on *my* terms." It's the ultimate form of pride, shrewdly cloaked in the garb of religion.

The Application

Everywhere false teachers defame the doctrines of the faith. It's rare to turn on the television or go to the movies and not see at least one Christian truth splayed and barbecued on the screen. In the media, on the college campus, in the workplace, our faith is under attack.

What is most disturbing, however, is the false teaching that has crept unnoticed into many of our churches, and even in our most venerated schools of theology. There even the most basic tenets of Christianity are denied: the Virgin Birth, the deity of Christ, His bodily resurrection, the existence of heaven and hell, the miracles of Jesus, the depravity of humankind, and the Second Coming. The impact of this teaching on the churches has been more of an erosion

---

6. Rienecker, *Linguistic Key to the Greek New Testament*, p. 804.

7. Barclay, *The Letters of John and Jude*, p. 180.

than an explosion. Inch by inch, the doctrinal foundation of many churches has all but washed away.

No longer can we assume that, once inside the walls of the church, we're safe from heresy. Joining voices with Jude, Peter warned:

> But false prophets also arose among the people, just as there will also be false teachers among you, who will secretly introduce destructive heresies, even denying the Master who bought them, bringing swift destruction upon themselves. And many will follow their sensuality, and because of them the way of the truth will be maligned. (2 Pet. 2:1–2)

Would you recognize false teaching if you saw it? If someone started maligning your faith, would you be strong enough to stand firm? Let's take seriously Jude's admonition to "contend earnestly for the faith." There's too much at stake to give up now.

Living Insights

"Did you know that Jesus never claimed to be God?"

"He didn't?"

"Nope. And He didn't really rise from the dead, either. The New Testament writers created the Resurrection and all the other miracle stories as sort of religious myths."

"So what we celebrate at Easter never happened?"

"Well, something happened, but it wasn't a physical resurrection. It was more of a spiritual awakening. Through His life and persecution, Jesus rose to a very high level of spiritual awareness. The disciples were so impressed with His experience that the best way they could describe it was with a story about a resurrection."

"You mean they lied to us?"

"No, no, no. They didn't lie. They simply hid the real meaning of Christianity within the story. The Bible is kind of like a picture-search puzzle. You have to look past the images on the surface to find the real truth."

"I don't get it. Did Jesus do what the gospel writers said He did or didn't He?"

"Whether or not the events really happened doesn't matter. What matters is how the stories transform you as you encounter

God through them and rise to higher levels of spiritual awareness yourself. Understand?"

"Well, it makes sense . . . I guess."

———————◆———————

This conversation is fictional, but the views expressed about Jesus and the Bible are very real in many churches today. You may have never heard them before, because most ministers who hold these views usually don't teach them so directly. Instead, by tinkering with definitions, they are able to preach about Christ yet deny His deity, His resurrection, His miracles, and His virgin birth, and no one knows the difference.

Spotting error is the first step to correcting it. Listen closely to what your pastor or teacher is saying. If something sounds a little strange to you, don't simply dismiss it. Take the time to pursue the matter. For as Paul encouraged Timothy,

> In pointing out these things [false doctrines] to the brethren, you will be a good servant of Christ Jesus, constantly nourished on the words of the faith and of the sound doctrine which you have been following. (1 Tim. 4:6)

Of course, we're not endorsing a witch hunt. It is possible to contend for the faith without being contentious, and we'll talk about how to do that in the next chapter. The point is, be aware . . . and be informed.

The following books, written in laymen's terms, will help you understand Bible doctrine from a conservative point of view. Select one and read through it. You'll be building a good foundation.

Enns, Paul. *The Moody Handbook of Theology.* Chicago, Ill.: Moody Press, 1989.

Erickson, Millard J. *Does It Matter What I Believe?* Grand Rapids, Mich.: Baker Book House, 1992.

Packer, J. I. *Knowing Christianity.* Wheaton, Ill.: Harold Shaw Publishers, 1995.

Ryrie, Charles C. *Basic Theology.* Wheaton, Ill.: Scripture Press Publications, Victor Books, 1986.

Shelley, Bruce L. *Theology for Ordinary People: What You Should Know to Make Sense out of Life*. Downers Grove, Ill.: InterVarsity Press, 1993. Revised edition of *Christian Theology in Plain Language* (1985).

Sproul, R. C. *Essential Truths of the Christian Faith*. Wheaton, Ill.: Tyndale House Publishers, 1992.

Stott, John R. W. *Basic Christianity*. 2d ed. 1971. Reprint, Grand Rapids, Mich.: William B. Eerdmans Publishing Co., 1989.

Swindoll, Charles R. *Growing Deep in the Christian Life*. Grand Rapids, Mich.: Zondervan Publishing House, 1995.

Walvoord, John F. *What We Believe: Discovering the Truths of Scripture*. Grand Rapids, Mich.: Discovery House Publishers, 1990.

Chapter 5

WHY BOTHER TO BATTLE?
Jude 5–16

A soldier hoists the flag and snaps a solemn salute. In the morning mist, a platoon double-times to a drill sergeant's husky cadence. The sound of clanking pans and sizzling bacon echoes through the cavernous mess hall. Another day of army life has begun.

The daily regimen on a military base is as well-trimmed as a new recruit's haircut. At 0800 hours, infantry personnel report to the rifle range for target practice. At 0830, a group of medics rehearse frontline first aid procedures. Nearby, in a maze of flourescent-bulbed offices, captains meet at 0900 to detail the complex logistics for field maneuvers. Throughout the day, corners are squared, boots are polished, and weapons are oiled.

The routine is an endless cycle of drilling and training for battles that everyone hopes will never happen. Yet, if an enemy threatens the nation's freedom, the well-trained soldier is ready to fight and even die so future generations can live in peace.

What's true for the military is also true for the church. We pray that enemies will never infiltrate our ranks with destructive doctrines. But if they do, we must be ready to fight for our beliefs.

In his little letter to the church, Jude rallies the troops with this cry: "Contend earnestly for the faith" (v. 3). And like a good field commander, he realizes the importance of stirring up our fighting spirit. In verses 5–16, Jude gives us a hard look at our enemy— a look that will motivate any Christian to get involved in the battle.

A Brief Review

As we saw in verse 4, the invaders who got Jude up in arms were twisting grace into licentiousness and denying Christ as Lord. This description seems to match a particular form of apostasy known as Gnosticism.

Gnosticism was an odd blend of Christianity and Greek philosophy. The Gnostics believed that we are saved by acquiring true "knowledge" (*gnosis*, in Greek) and that our bodies are evil and our spirits are good. According to theologian Millard Erickson, this teaching led to two extremes:

Whereas some Gnostics drew the conclusion that, the body being evil, a strict asceticism should be practiced, others concluded that what is done with the body is spiritually irrelevant, and hence engaged in licentious behavior.[1]

Apparently, the latter group of Gnostics had infiltrated the church, "claiming to be so Spirit-filled that there was no room for law in their Christian lives. . . . Those who fussed about sexual purity seemed to them astonishingly naive."[2] They also taught strange doctrines about Christ. They denied His humanity, saying that He only seemed to have a body. And they denied His uniqueness, teaching that He represented only one of many stages on the way to God.[3]

Having established a beachhead in the church, the Gnostics were striking at the heart of the Christian faith. Like a Paul Revere sounding the alarm, Jude rouses the troops. The enemy is upon us! Now is the time for action!

Reasons to Fight

Bolstering their confidence, Jude writes, "Now I desire to remind you, though *you know all things once for all*" (v. 5a, emphasis added). They don't have to seek the special, mystical knowledge of the Gnostics. At their fingertips are all the riches of wisdom they need (compare 1 Cor. 2:10–16; Eph. 1:8b–9, 17; James 1:5; 3:17). Jude draws upon their store of knowledge to list four reasons for battling the enemy.

Because Their Doom Is Certain

The first reason is that the apostate faces a certain doom.

Now I desire to remind you, though you know all things once for all, that the Lord, after saving a people out of the land of Egypt, subsequently destroyed those who did not believe. And angels who did not keep their own domain, but abandoned their

---

1. Millard J. Erickson, *Christian Theology* (Grand Rapids, Mich.: Baker Book House, 1985), p. 1197.

2. Michael Green, *The Second Epistle General of Peter and the General Epistle of Jude,* The Tyndale New Testament Commentaries Series (Grand Rapids, Mich.: William B. Eerdmans Publishing Co., 1968), p. 181.

3. See William Barclay, *The Letters of John and Jude,* rev. ed., The Daily Study Bible series (Philadelphia, Pa.: Westminster Press, 1976), p. 180.

proper abode, He has kept in eternal bonds under darkness for the judgment of the great day. Just as Sodom and Gomorrah and the cities around them, since they in the same way as these indulged in gross immorality and went after strange flesh, are exhibited as an example, in undergoing the punishment of eternal fire. (Jude 5–7)

Jude presents a triad of examples: (1) unbelieving Israelites, (2) fallen angels, and (3) the wicked people of Sodom and Gomorrah. Let's take a closer look at each of these.

Just like the faithless Israelites who refused to enter the Promised Land after God had led them out of Egypt (see Num. 13–14), so apostates are destined to die in the wilderness of their unbelief.

And just like the fallen angels, whom God judged (see Gen. 6:1–4; Isa. 14:12–17), so these arrogant and audacious false teachers will suffer God's wrath in the coming day of judgment.

And just like the citizens of Sodom and Gomorrah, whom God destroyed in flames because of their sexual perversions (see Gen. 19), so the wicked apostates will face God's fiery condemnation.

The implication of Jude's message is clear: Don't sympathize with those whom God condemns. Why hear them out or entertain the idea of following them when their path has led *them* to death and will just as surely take us there too? It's absurd to think we'd find the way of life in those who are spiritually dead. If they attack what we believe, we must be prepared to fight for the purity of God's message. It's a matter of eternal life or death.

Because Their Tongues Are Blasphemous

Another reason to confront the false teachers is because of their blasphemous tongues.

> Yet in the same manner these men, also by dreaming, defile the flesh, and reject authority, and revile angelic majesties. But Michael the archangel, when he disputed with the devil and argued about the body of Moses, did not dare pronounce against him a railing judgment, but said, "The Lord rebuke you." But these men revile the things which they do not understand; and the things which they know by instinct, like unreasoning animals, by these things they are destroyed. (Jude 8–10)

We can usually distinguish false teachers by their *irreverent cynicism toward things that are sacred*. Their perceptions and ideas are not shaped by divine truth but by their own "dreams" and imaginings and faulty opinions. Their speculations form their beliefs, which are tailor-made to accommodate sexual immorality. They then become their own "authority"—to the point that they don't even respect God's superior, holy angels (v. 8).

In verse 9, Jude illustrates the magnitude of their blasphemies through a story from the Assumption of Moses, an apocryphal book familiar to his readers.[4] According to the account, the archangel Michael was sent to bury Moses' body, but Lucifer intercepted him, claiming the body was his. Instead of showing disrespect toward Lucifer, Michael left the matter with the Judge of all creatures, saying, "The Lord rebuke you." The point is this: If Michael weighed his words carefully when addressing the wickedest of angels, how presumptuous it was for the apostates to rail against righteous angels!

Another characteristic of apostates is their *irreverent reviling of matters they don't understand*. They live by sight, not faith; so if something cannot be comprehended or explained rationally, they reject it. For example, if they can't neatly define a certain doctrine, such as the Trinity, they mock it. There is no place, and certainly no respect, for mystery in the mind of many apostates.

A third characteristic of false teachers is their *irreverent pursuit of animalistic desires*. Recklessly riding the downward spiral of humanism, apostates consider themselves captains of their own destinies. They therefore toss aside all restraints that don't suit them and eagerly supply whatever their raging appetites demand. Ironically, in their pursuit of freedom, they become like animals, caged by their own desires.

Francis Schaeffer, in his book *How Should We Then Live?*, strips away humanism's veneer to reveal where it's really headed.

> Humanism [has] no way to find the universal in the
> areas of meaning and values. As my son, Franky, put
> it, "Humanism has changed the Twenty-third Psalm:
>   They began—I am my shepherd

---

4. By citing familiar extrabiblical passages, Jude was merely adding punch and relevance to his points, much like Paul did when he quoted the Greek poet Aratus in his address to the intellectuals at Mars Hill (see Acts 17:28). Even non-inspired works can carry elements of truth.

Then—Sheep are my shepherd
Then—Everything is my shepherd
Finally—Nothing is my shepherd."
There is a death wish inherent in humanism—the impulsive drive to beat to death the base which made our freedoms and our culture possible.[5]

Because Their Religion Is Empty

We should also confront apostates because their religion is empty. It is shot full of so many errors that all the living water of Christ has drained out. Jude's three-pronged indictment in verse 11 illustrates the sort of heresies the apostates in his day taught:

> Woe to them! For they have gone the way of Cain, and for pay they have rushed headlong into the error of Balaam, and perished in the rebellion of Korah.

What exactly is Jude alluding to in these examples? First, the false teachers followed "the way of Cain" by endorsing a religion that offers God the fruit of human works rather than the innocent blood of a substitutionary sacrifice (see Gen. 4:1–7; Heb. 9:22; 11:4).

Motivated by greed, they rushed into "the error of Balaam," who set out to sell his prophecies against Israel to the Moabites, until the Lord stopped him (see Num. 22; Deut. 23:3–4; Neh. 13:2; 2 Pet. 2:15–16).[6]

Finally, they spearheaded a "rebellion of Korah." Korah was a Levite who led a mutiny against Moses and Aaron. In his pride, Korah presumed that he could approach a holy God without God's chosen mediators. Because of his defiance, God commanded the earth to swallow up him and his followers in an earthquake (see Num. 16:1–33). Similarly, the apostates defied the authority of Christ and the apostles, God's chosen vessels of truth.[7]

---

5. Francis A. Schaeffer, *How Should We Then Live?* (Westchester, Ill.: Good News Publishers, Crossway Books, 1976), p. 226.

6. Balaam found another way to undermine Israel's faith. He lured the men into sexual immorality and Baal worship at Peor (see Num. 25:2; 31:15–16; Rev. 2:14). Teaching heresy is one thing, but teaching people to sin—that's the worst treachery of all (see Luke 17:1–2). This was exactly what the apostates were doing in the church.

7. No matter how reasonable its words or winsome its ways, apostasy is diametrically opposed to Christ. Instead of the *way* of Christ, there is the way of Cain. Instead of the *truth* of Christ, there is the error of Balaam. Instead of the *life* of Christ, there is the death of Korah.

Jude's not finished with his indictments. In verses 12–13, he pummels the false teachers with a flurry of charges:

> These men are those who are hidden reefs in your love feasts when they feast with you without fear, caring for themselves; clouds without water, carried along by winds; autumn trees without fruit, doubly dead, uprooted; wild waves of the sea, casting up their own shame like foam; wandering stars, for whom the black darkness has been reserved forever.

This montage of images brings to life Jude's character sketch of the heinous false teachers. They are as treacherous as hidden reefs, their selfishness shipwrecking others' faith in the most sacred area—the Lord's Supper. Like clouds without water, they have nothing real to offer a thirsting soul. As fruitless, uprooted trees, they can't nourish the spirit's deepest hunger, and their own source of life is as dried up and eternally dead as upturned roots. They are as destructive as wild ocean waves, leaving a foam of immorality on the shore for everyone to see. And like "wandering" or shooting stars, which shine "briefly, and then vanish without producing light or giving direction,"[8] they lead others astray and then disappear in the darkness of judgment.

Because Their Ways Are Godless

In explaining his fourth reason to oppose the apostates, Jude launches an all-out, frontal attack:

> And about these also Enoch, in the seventh generation from Adam, prophesied, saying, "Behold, the Lord came with many thousands of His holy ones, to execute judgment upon all, and to convict all the ungodly of all their ungodly deeds which they have done in an ungodly way, and of all the harsh things which ungodly sinners have spoken against Him." These are grumblers, finding fault, following after their own lusts; they speak arrogantly, flattering people for the sake of gaining an advantage. (vv. 14–16)

8. Edward C. Pentecost, "Jude," in *The Bible Knowledge Commentary*, New Testament edition, ed. John F. Walvoord and Roy B. Zuck (Wheaton, Ill.: Scripture Press Publications, Victor Books, 1983), p. 922.

Jude quotes another popular apocryphal book, Enoch, to get across his point. These false teachers may put on a godly show, but unmasked, they're crooks. We can see the lips sneering contemptuously in complaint, a faultfinding finger pointed in ridicule, eyes glinting with lust, an eyebrow lifted in arrogance, the empty smile of a manipulative flatterer. They are the exact opposite of what they say they are—they're *un*godly. And God will judge them according to their evil deeds.

A Balanced Response

Jude's purpose has been to get our blood boiling against apostates. Has it worked? Are you ready to take them on? Before you do, beware. There's always a danger of your righteous indignation boiling over and spewing out as uncontrolled hostility. Before you know it, calm confrontations can quickly explode into name-calling and shouting matches. And then nobody wins.

How can we fight passionately for the faith without losing our heads? The key is to be thoroughly prepared. The most persuasive argument in any debate is the truth; so use it. Know where you stand doctrinally. Know where your enemy stands too. And, finally, don't be afraid to take a stand. You may be the one flickering flame in the darkness, the only voice in a crowd of dissenters . . . but you're never alone. God's Spirit and His Word are with you all the way.

Living Insights

Great damage can result from small beginnings. For instance, the charred remains of a forest fire show the destructive power of one, tiny spark. A small amount of rust can eat away a sturdy iron fence. Or a little crack in the foundation can cause a whole building to collapse. Paul put it this way: "A little leaven leavens the whole lump of dough," (Gal. 5:9). In the same way, a little false doctrine can destroy an entire church.

What can we do to protect our churches and ministries from the small heresies that grow into large tragedies? We can be aware and informed, as we mentioned in the last Living Insight. Then, if we see a subtle invasion of false doctrine, we can follow the procedures for confrontation that Jesus outlined in Matthew 18:15–17.

Let's say that your adult Sunday school leader begins to challenge the authority of Scripture. Perhaps he or she questions the Virgin Birth or the miracles of Christ. What's your first step, according to verse 15?

_____

_____

_____

Although sometimes we need to check with someone else to see if we're viewing the situation accurately, there are times when we merely complain to everyone but the person we're complaining about. That approach usually just fans the fire into an unnecessary blaze. Many times, there was a simple misunderstanding, and the issue can be doused quietly.

However, if the leader continues to challenge the Scripture, what do you do next (v. 16)?

_____

_____

_____

And if that doesn't stop the false teaching, what do you do (v. 17)?

_____

_____

_____

When you "tell it to the church," the best place to start is with the leadership. They will want to talk to the person and, perhaps, publish a statement concerning the church's position on a certain doctrine. If all else fails, the church board may have to ask the teacher to leave the church.

No one likes church battles; they're messy and painful. But when the purity of the truth is at stake, they are essential. We must be firm in our stand for the faith—not with a boastful and contentious spirit, but with humility and courage.

Chapter 6

GET YOUR ACT TOGETHER!

Jude 17–25

As the war against Hitler raged in Europe, Winston Churchill, in his first statement as prime minister, addressed the House of Commons on May 13, 1940, with these words:

> I have nothing to offer but blood, toil, tears and sweat.[1]

That blood and toil, those tears and drops of sweat were put to the test when British ships and boats rescued more than 300,000 Allied troops who were cut off from land retreat by the Germans at Dunkirk. Thirty thousand French and British soldiers were killed or taken prisoner, but still that tenacious bulldog of the British Empire stood his ground:

> We shall not flag or fail. We shall go on to the end.
> We shall fight in France, we shall fight on the seas
> and oceans, we shall fight with growing confidence
> and growing strength in the air, we shall defend our
> island, whatever the cost may be, we shall fight on
> the beaches, we shall fight on the landing grounds,
> we shall fight in the fields and in the streets, we shall
> fight in the hills; we shall never surrender.[2]

Churchill's words ring with the fixed resolve of a man contending earnestly for the preservation of his country. With similar determination, Jude exhorts us to "contend earnestly for the faith" (Jude 3). The enemy storming our shores is apostasy; what hangs in the balance is the preservation of truth and morality. In verses 17–25, Jude makes a final appeal to the soldiers of the faith who are in the midst of a raging battle against the onslaught of false teachers.

A Serious Situation

Jude worried that his readers might become spiritual casualties—

---

1. Sir Winston Churchill, as quoted in *Bartlett's Familiar Quotations*, 16th ed., ed. Justin Kaplan, (Boston, Mass.: Little, Brown and Co., 1992), p. 620.

2. Churchill, in a speech to the House of Commons, June 4, 1940, as quoted in *Bartlett's Familiar Quotations*, p. 620.

and for good reason. They were already under attack from the Romans, who were stepping up their persecutions. Now they had to deal with the insidious assaults of the apostates (see 2 Tim. 3:6–9; 4:3–4). Jude fervently pleaded with them to fight for their beliefs.

Although our situation has changed since the first century, the issue is just as serious. Plenty of enemies of Christ lurk outside and inside the church, waiting to assail our faith. That's why, as much as ever, we need to build around us a protective fortress of truth.

In the remainder of his postcard, Jude focuses on the weary soldiers who are trying to fortify their lives with the truth. Let's listen closely to the commander's encouraging final instructions.

Final Instructions for the Troops

Jude issues at least four commands in the closing verses: remember, keep, have mercy, and save.

Remember the Training Manual

> But you, beloved, ought to remember the words that were spoken beforehand by the apostles of our Lord Jesus Christ, that they were saying to you, "In the last time there shall be mockers, following after their own ungodly lusts." These are the ones who cause divisions, worldly-minded, devoid of the Spirit. (Jude 17–19)

In the training manual of Scripture, the apostles warned us about false teachers. They come with the territory of living in the last days (see Acts 20:28–30; 1 Tim. 4:1–2; 2 Pet. 3:3–4). By expecting them, we're less likely to become paralyzed and disillusioned when they invade our church. We take away their surprise advantage, and if we can spot them under their camouflage, the battle is half over. Jude gives us five characteristics to look for. Apostates are:

- *Mockers.* With cynical jabs, they ridicule the doctrines of the faith and scoff at the authority of Scripture.

- *Immoral.* Corrupt theology almost always decays into corrupt morals. Once apostates cut loose the anchor of Scripture, they freely follow the winds of their own lusts without remorse.

- *Divisive.* With an elitist air, they put themselves above the leaders of the church and sow seeds of discord and doubt—a critical word about the pastor, a skeptical remark about Christ.

- *Worldly-minded.* Like the Pharisees, they boast in their separateness and spirituality. They claim that they are not "bound to the restrictions and inhibitions of ordinary Christians."[3] In actuality, Jude says, their mind-set is entirely worldly. They are ruled by their natural desires.

- *Without the Spirit.* There is a telling reason for their worldly-mindedness: they are "devoid of the Spirit." They are fake Christians (see Rom. 8:9).

Keep in Shape

Knowing what the training manual says about apostates is helpful, but it's not enough. Jude gives us some action steps to follow in verses 20–21.

> But you, beloved, building yourselves up on your most holy faith; praying in the Holy Spirit; keep yourselves in the love of God, waiting anxiously for the mercy of our Lord Jesus Christ to eternal life.

Jude's imperative to "keep yourselves in the love of God" brings to mind Jesus' command:

> "Just as the Father has loved Me, I have also loved you; abide in My love." (John 15:9)

Apart from Christ, we can do nothing (v. 5). His love must flow in us and through us to others, even to our enemies. Otherwise, in the battle, our hearts will grow cold and we will become hardened fighters, full of hate and hostility.

How do we cultivate His love in our lives? First, by building ourselves up in the faith. This requires that we study the Bible and the doctrines that have been handed down through the centuries. As we learn about Christ, we grow in our love for Him, and we add stones of knowledge to our wall of faith. When the enemy fires false doctrine at us, the arrows simply bounce off because we know they aren't true.

3. Michael Green, *The Second Epistle General of Peter and the General Epistle of Jude*, The Tyndale New Testament Commentaries series (Grand Rapids, Mich.: William B. Eerdmans Publishing Co., 1968), p. 183.

Recall for a moment the essentials of the faith listed on page 15. Are there any holes in your understanding of those doctrines? Any points of weakness? Any slumping walls that an enemy could easily breach and start dismantling your faith?

Second, the mortar that holds our knowledge in place is "praying in the Spirit" (v. 20). What exactly does that mean? It begins with an admission of our weakness. We can't pray as we should because we are limited in our spiritual understanding and power. That's where the Holy Spirit comes in. "He intercedes for the saints according to the will of God" (Rom. 8:26–27). By admitting our weakness, depending on the Holy Spirit to bridge the gap between us and God, and then submitting to God's will—whatever that may prove to be—we are *praying in the Spirit*. God's thoughts become our thoughts and His ways, our ways (see Isa. 55:8–9).

We start in weakness, but through prayer, we end in God's strength. It's amazing how the Enemy's intimidating threats lose their power when we commit ourselves and the battle to the Lord. We are never so strong as when we are on our knees.

Finally, we stay in His love by keeping the torch of hope lit within our hearts. Like soldiers who dream of the day when they will return home to the warm embrace of their families and loved ones, we anxiously look forward to that day when we will see our Savior face-to-face. At that moment, all our doubts and fears will fade into the eternal joy of His embrace.

Have Mercy on the War-torn

Good soldiers not only watch out for themselves, they also take care of each other—particularly the wounded. Under the barrage of false teaching, some will waver in their faith. Their flame of hope nearly extinguished, they will stagger on the battlefield and collapse. How should the stronger soldiers respond? By jabbing them with criticism? By abandoning them in disgust? Of course not. Jude tells us, "Have mercy on some, who are doubting" (v. 22).

The Greek text for this verse is uncertain. Some manuscripts read *mercy*, while others read *confront* or *convince*. The latter seems more likely. The idea is to patiently convince the doubting person of the truth (see Gal. 6:1; 1 Thess. 5:14).

Save the Defectors

If the doubter refuses to be convinced, he or she may defect or "apostasize." All is not lost, however. Jude exhorts us, "save others, snatching them out of the fire" (v. 23a). By going to the enemy, these defectors have stumbled into a building on fire. Rescuing them requires quick and determined action. We may have to pull them out by their collars, but we will save their lives from destruction (see James 5:19–20).[4]

If they still resist, Jude gives us this instruction:

> On some have mercy with fear, hating even the garment polluted by the flesh. (Jude 23b)

Instead of despising them as traitors or throwing stones of judgment, we are to pity them with fear. We, too, might be in the clutches of the apostates were it not for the grace of God. Their tragedy should stir within us a passion for holiness. Instead of hating them, we should hate the sin that destroyed them and everything associated with the sin—"the garment polluted by the flesh." No doubt, Jude pulls the image out of the book of Leviticus, in which the priests were to burn the polluted garments of a leper because they carried the disease (Lev. 13:47–59). Whatever carries the disease of their apostasy, we must not touch.

Final Benediction for the Troops

Jude's closing benediction communicates God's protection during today's battle and the battles to come. With the stirring rhetoric of Churchill, he calls out to the troops:

> Now to Him who is able to keep you from stumbling, and to make you stand in the presence of His glory blameless with great joy, to the only God our Savior, through Jesus Christ our Lord, be glory, majesty, dominion and authority, before all time and now and forever. Amen. (Jude 24–25)

The word *stumbling* is *aptaistos* in Greek. It was used in a literal sense to describe a sure-footed horse that does not stumble.[5] In this world, chuckholes of temptation and loose rocks of false doctrine fill our path. Only the Lord can give us the moral stability and spiritual wisdom to keep our footing firm.

---

4. Apostasized believers will not lose their salvation but will suffer the Lord's discipline, which may include physical death. At the believer's judgment, all their works will be destroyed, and they will suffer great loss (see 1 Cor. 3:10–15).

5. Green, *Peter and Jude*, p. 190.

But that is not all God can do. He can make us stand confidently before His righteous throne, with great joy, not with fearful trembling. Why? Because of the sure platform of Christ's atonement. With God as our Savior, we have nothing to fear, in this world or the next.

Jude sends us marching into battle singing the praises of God, confident in His mighty arm of salvation. As we go our way, steadfastly facing the opposition within the church and the persecution without, surely the "angelic majesties" will look down upon us and say: "This was their finest hour."[6]

Living Insights

Defection. It can happen to anyone, even the most loyal soldiers. Charles Swindoll recalls the tragic story of one young man who went AWOL in the battle of faith.

> He was one of those ten-talented teenagers who was still in high school but showed the promise and maturity of being far beyond his years. . . . We began to have time together. We shared meals. We shared our home. Cynthia and I took him with us as we would go from place to place, even in travel. And he really won our hearts, and we his. . . .
>
> He had a number of scholarships available. And he chose a school nearby because he didn't want to lose touch with me. And he began to grow for two years at this school. Then he realized, to get the kind of pre-seminary education he wanted, he'd have to go to a better university. So he transferred. And he spent his junior and senior year in a school of an altogether different persuasion. And two things happened that were tragic. First, he began to tolerate a philosophy that was not biblical. It made good sense . . . So he imbibed the philosophy of secular humanism. . . . And second, he married a girl who was neck-deep in it. And with her, he got the literature and the idols of her life and began to worship both.
>
> I had lost touch with him for about twelve, fifteen

---

6. Churchill, *Bartlett's Familiar Quotations*, p. 620.

months. And then he came back, scooted into the town where he was going to go to school, and we met. And I noticed some things were different. He didn't sound the same. Obviously, his eye contact wasn't what it had been. Didn't have that heart for God that he had always had, that beautiful sense of humor that was so delightful to be around. But there was a hardness now, there was a callousness. Erosion had happened. . . .

. . . And I began to watch him and spend a little time with him, though he avoided me more than ever. . . . His first year [in seminary] was tolerated. His second year was misery. He was told not to come back his third year. He gave me a lot of his books . . . even some of his writings, which were marvelous, but he no longer agreed with those things.

And, by and by, he was under the constant care of a psychiatrist. His marriage got shaky. And the last encounter I had with him was at a restaurant where I sat eyeball-to-eyeball with a living apostate, a guy whom I had nurtured and poured life and time and energy and love into who had bought the system.[7]

Do you know anyone like this young man? Someone who was in the trenches, fighting for the faith, but over time began to show signs of doubt, then cynicism, then defiance? Your friend is not the person you used to know. Doesn't talk the same or act the same. Dresses different. Looks different. How can you get him or her back again?

Jude says the first step is to confront, to try to convince them of the truth they have spurned (v. 22). Sometimes we associate confronting with "setting someone straight." But one-sided confrontations usually make people defensive and more determined to justify their position. The best way to begin confronting is by listening. Try to understand thoroughly your friend's thinking and, especially, his or her feelings.

Next, schedule a meeting with your friend. Determine ahead of time what approach you're going to take and what your attitude

---

7. Charles R. Swindoll, from the sermon transcript, "Get Your Act Together!" preached September 25, 1977, at the First Evangelical Free Church of Fullerton, California, pp. 24–27. A postscript to this story is that after years of wandering, this man finally came home to the faith.

will be. How do 1 Thessalonians 5:14; Galatians 6:1–2; and Hebrews 12:12–13 help prepare for this meeting?

You may spend several meetings with your friend at this stage. If there is no change of heart, you may be ready to go to the next step: rescue. Your purpose now is to make the strongest emotional appeal possible. You may want to write a letter and read it to your friend.[8] You may want to get other mutual friends involved.

If your friend remains hardened, there's not much more you can say. Only one step remains: "have mercy with fear" (Jude 23). In other words, keep loving, keep humble, and keep praying.

---

8. We recommend Gary Smalley and John Trent's book *The Language of Love* (Pomona, Calif.: Focus on the Family Publishing, 1988), to help you frame your thoughts into an emotionally powerful appeal.

Books for
Probing Further

Before you bundle up these postcards and tuck them away, thumb through them one final time, so the images make an imprint on your memory.

- Philemon pictures a runaway slave appealing to his former owner for forgiveness.

- Second John depicts a woman so eager to be hospitable that she sheltered the enemy—the false teachers.

- Third John, on the other hand, cameos three men, one of whom made it a habit to rudely refuse hospitality to the true teachers of the church.

- On the bottom of the stack, Jude exposes the false teachers and admonishes us to "contend earnestly for the faith."

Put together, these postcards provide a revealing collage of the first-century church. But the pictures are as vivid and unfaded as if they were taken yesterday, and the applications as personal as if addressed to each of us individually.

For example, do you need to ask forgiveness from a Philemon and restore a severed relationship? Do you need to reach out with grace and reinstate an Onesimus into your life and heart?

Are you like the lady in 2 John, naive about the people you welcome into your home, perhaps through television or radio? Are you inadvertently aiding and abetting the Enemy by listening to misguided or false teachers or by receiving their literature?

Perhaps, like Diotrephes in 3 John, you're at the other extreme. Maybe the door to your home and heart stays dead-bolted, to the extent that the genuinely good and honest teachers of the gospel are turned away brusquely. Do you need to unlatch that door, welcoming and honoring those guests?

Like the recipients of Jude's urgent note, have certain dangerous people "crept in unnoticed" to your church or even your mind? Or like the apostates themselves, is there hidden theological or moral corruption that needs to be brought into the open? What do you need to do to contend for your true, eternally significant faith?

Postcards, though small, can make a big impact, can't they? If these brief letters have struck a responsive chord in your heart, the following resources can help you make their truth part of the living letter of your life.

Barclay, William. *The Letters of John and Jude*. Rev. ed. The Daily Study Bible series. Philadelphia, Pa.: Westminster Press, 1976.

———. *The Letters to Timothy, Titus, and Philemon*. Rev. ed. The Daily Study Bible series. Philadelphia, Pa.: Westminster Press, 1975.

Green, Michael. *The Second Epistle General of Peter and the General Epistle of Jude*. The Tyndale New Testament Commentaries. Grand Rapids, Mich.: William B. Eerdmans Publishing Co., 1968.

Horton, Michael, ed. *The Agony of Deceit*. Chicago, Ill.: Moody Press, 1990.

Little, Paul E. *Know Why You Believe*. Rev. ed. Wheaton, Ill.: Scripture Press Publications, Victor Books, 1987.

Sproul, R. C. *Reason to Believe: A Response to Common Objections to Christianity*. Grand Rapids, Mich.: Zondervan Publishing House, 1978.

Smedes, Lewis B. *Forgive and Forget: Healing the Hurts We Don't Deserve*. New York, N.Y.: Simon and Schuster, Pocket Books, 1984.

Stott, J. R. W. *The Epistles of John*. The Tyndale New Testament Commentaries. 1964. Reprint, Grand Rapids, Mich.: William B. Eerdmans Publishing Co., 1969.

Some of these books may be out of print and available only through a library. For those currently available, please contact your local Christian bookstore. Books by Charles R. Swindoll may be obtained through Insight for Living. IFL also offers some books by other authors—please note the ordering information that follows and contact the office that serves you.

ORDERING INFORMATION

NEW TESTAMENT POSTCARDS
Cassette Tapes and Study Guide

This Bible study guide was designed to be used independently or in conjunction with the broadcast of Chuck Swindoll's taped messages which are listed below. If you would like to order cassette tapes or further copies of this study guide, please see the information given below and the order form provided at the end of this guide.

		U.S.	Canada
NTP	Study guide	$ 4.95	$ 6.50
NTPCS	Cassette series, includes all individual tapes, album cover, and one complimentary study guide	22.00	24.50
NTP 1–3	Individual cassettes, includes messages A and B	6.00	7.48

Prices are subject to change without notice.

NTP 1-A: *A Postcard to Philemon*—Philemon
B: *A Postcard to a Lady and Her Kids*—2 John

NTP 2-A: *A Postcard of Candid Truth*—3 John
B: *The Acts of the Apostates*—Jude 1–4

NTP 3-A: *Why Bother to Battle?*—Jude 5–16
B: *Get Your Act Together!*—Jude 17–25

HOW TO ORDER BY PHONE OR FAX
(Credit card orders only)

Web site: http://www.insight.org

United States: 1-800-772-8888 or FAX (714) 575-5684, 24 hours a day, 7 days a week

Canada: 1-800-663-7639 or FAX (604) 532-7173, 24 hours a day, 7 days a week.

Australia and the South Pacific: (03) 9872-4606 or FAX (03) 9874-8890 from 8:00 A.M. to 5:00 P.M., Monday through Friday

Other International Locations: call the International Ordering Services Department in the United States at (714) 575-5000 from 8:00 A.M. to 4:30 P.M., Pacific time, Monday through Friday
FAX (714) 575-5683 anytime, day or night

HOW TO ORDER BY MAIL

United States
- Mail to: Mail Center
    Insight for Living
    Post Office Box 69000
    Anaheim, CA 92817-0900
- Sales tax: California residents add 7.75%.
- Shipping and handling charges must be added to each order. See chart on order form for amount.
- Payment: personal checks, money orders, credit cards (Visa, MasterCard, Discover Card, and American Express). No invoices or COD orders available.
- $10 fee for *any* returned check.

Canada
- Mail to: Insight for Living Ministries
    Post Office Box 2510
    Vancouver, BC V6B 3W7
- Sales tax: please add 7% GST. British Columbia residents also add 7% sales tax (on tapes or cassette series).
- Shipping and handling charges must be added to each order. See chart on order form for amount.
- Payment: personal cheques, money orders, credit cards (Visa, Master-Card). No invoices or COD orders available.
- Delivery: approximately four weeks.

Australia and the South Pacific
- Mail to: Insight for Living, Inc.
    GPO Box 2823 EE
    Melbourne, Victoria 3001, Australia
- Shipping: add 25% to the total order.
- Delivery: approximately four to six weeks.
- Payment: personal checks payable in Australian funds, international money orders, or credit cards (Visa, MasterCard, and Bankcard).

United Kingdom and Europe
- Mail to: Insight for Living
  c/o Trans World Radio
  Post Office Box 1020
  Bristol BS99 1XS
  England, United Kingdom
- Shipping: add 25% to the total order.
- Delivery: approximately four to six weeks.
- Payment: cheques payable in sterling pounds or credit cards (Visa, MasterCard, and American Express).

Other International Locations
- Mail to: International Processing Services Department
  Insight for Living
  Post Office Box 69000
  Anaheim, CA 92817-0900
- Shipping and delivery time: please see chart that follows.
- Payment: personal checks payable in U.S. funds, international money orders, or credit cards (Visa, MasterCard, and American Express).

Type of Shipping	Postage Cost	Delivery
Surface	10% of total order*	6 to 10 weeks
Airmail	25% of total order*	under 6 weeks

Use U.S. price as a base.

Our Guarantee: Your complete satisfaction is our top priority here at Insight for Living. If you're not completely satisfied with anything you order, please return it for full credit, a refund, or a replacement, as *you* prefer.

Insight for Living Catalog: The Insight for Living catalog features study guides, tapes, and books by a variety of Christian authors. To obtain a free copy, call us at the numbers listed above.

Order Form
United States, Australia, and Other International Locations
(Canadian residents please use order form on reverse side.)

NTPCS represents the entire *New Testament Postcards* series in a special album cover, while NTP 1–3 are the individual tapes included in the series. NTP represents this study guide, should you desire to order additional copies.

NTP	Study guide	$ 4.95 ea.
NTPCS	Cassette series, includes all individual tapes, album cover, and one complimentary study guide	22.00
NTP 1–3	Individual cassettes, includes messages A and B	6.00 ea.

Product Code	Product Description	Quantity	Unit Price	Total
			$	$

Amount of Order	First Class	UPS		
			Order Total	
			UPS ❏ First Class ❏ *Shipping and handling must be added. See chart for charges.*	
$ 7.50 and under	1.00	4.00		
$ 7.51 to 12.50	1.50	4.25	Subtotal	
$12.51 to 25.00	3.50	4.50	California Residents—Sales Tax *Add 7.75% of subtotal.*	
$25.01 to 35.00	4.50	4.75	**Non-United States Residents** *Australia and Europe add 25%. All other locations: U.S. price plus 10% surface postage or 25% airmail.*	
$35.01 to 60.00	5.50	5.25		
$60.00 and over	6.50	5.75		

Rush shipping and Fourth Class are also available. Please call for details.

Gift to Insight for Living *Tax-deductible in the United States.*	
Total Amount Due *Please do not send cash.*	$

Prices are subject to change without notice.

Payment by: ❏ Check or money order payable to Insight for Living ❏ Credit card

(Circle one):   Visa   MasterCard   Discover Card   American Express   Bankcard

Number _____

Expiration Date _____   Signature _____ (In Australia)

We cannot process your credit card purchase without your signature.

Name _____

Address _____

City _____   State _____

Zip Code _____   Country _____

Telephone (____) _____   Radio Station ____ ____ ____ ____

If questions arise concerning your order, we may need to contact you.

Mail this order form to the Mail Center at one of these addresses:

Insight for Living
Post Office Box 69000, Anaheim, CA 92817-0900

Insight for Living, Inc.
GPO Box 2823 EE, Melbourne, VIC 3001, Australia

ECFA
MEMBER

Order Form
Canadian Residents

(Residents of the United States, Australia, and other international locations, please use order form on reverse side.)

NTPCS represents the entire *New Testament Postcards* series in a special album cover, while NTP 1–3 are the individual tapes included in the series. NTP represents this study guide, should you desire to order additional copies.

NTP	Study guide	$ 6.50 ea.
NTPCS	Cassette series, includes all individual tapes, album cover, and one complimentary study guide	24.50
NTP 1–3	Individual cassettes, includes messages A and B	7.48 ea.

Product Code	Product Description	Quantity	Unit Price	Total
			$	$

Subtotal	
Add 7% GST	
British Columbia Residents *Add 7% sales tax on individual tapes or cassette series.*	
Shipping *Shipping and handling must be added. See chart for charges.*	
Gift to Insight for Living Ministries *Tax-deductible in Canada.*	
Total Amount Due *Please do not send cash.*	$

Amount of Order	Canada Post
Orders to $10.00	2.00
$10.01 to 30.00	3.50
$30.01 to 50.00	5.00
$50.01 to 99.99	7.00
$100 and over	Free

Loomis Courier is also available.
Please call for details.

Prices are subject to change without notice.

Payment by: ❏ Cheque or money order payable to Insight for Living Ministries
❏ Credit card

(Circle one): Visa   MasterCard   Number _____

Expiration Date _____   Signature _____
We cannot process your credit card purchase without your signature.

Name _____

Address _____

City _____   Province _____

Postal Code _____   Country _____

Telephone (___) _____   Radio Station ____ ____ ____ ____
If questions arise concerning your order, we may need to contact you.

Mail this order form to the Processing Services Department at the following address:

Insight for Living Ministries
Post Office Box 2510
Vancouver, BC, Canada V6B 3W7

Order Form
United States, Australia, and Other International Locations
(Canadian residents please use order form on reverse side.)

NTPCS represents the entire *New Testament Postcards* series in a special album cover, while NTP 1–3 are the individual tapes included in the series. NTP represents this study guide, should you desire to order additional copies.

NTP	Study guide	$ 4.95 ea.
NTPCS	Cassette series,	22.00
	includes all individual tapes, album cover, and one complimentary study guide	
NTP 1–3	Individual cassettes,	6.00 ea.
	includes messages A and B	

Product Code	Product Description	Quantity	Unit Price	Total
			$	$

Amount of Order	First Class	UPS		
			Order Total	
			UPS ❏ First Class ❏ *Shipping and handling must be added. See chart for charges.*	
$ 7.50 and under	1.00	4.00		
$ 7.51 to 12.50	1.50	4.25	Subtotal	
$12.51 to 25.00	3.50	4.50	**California Residents—Sales Tax** *Add 7.75% of subtotal.*	
$25.01 to 35.00	4.50	4.75		
$35.01 to 60.00	5.50	5.25	**Non-United States Residents** *Australia and Europe add 25%. All other locations: U.S. price plus 10% surface postage or 25% airmail.*	
$60.00 and over	6.50	5.75		

Rush shipping and Fourth Class are also available. Please call for details.

Gift to Insight for Living *Tax-deductible in the United States.*	
Total Amount Due *Please do not send cash.*	$

Prices are subject to change without notice.

Payment by: ❏ Check or money order payable to Insight for Living   ❏ Credit card
(Circle one):   Visa   MasterCard   Discover Card   American Express   Bankcard

Number _____
(In Australia)

Expiration Date _____   Signature _____
We cannot process your credit card purchase without your signature.

Name _____

Address _____

City _____   State _____

Zip Code _____   Country _____

Telephone (___) _____   Radio Station ____ ____ ____ ____
If questions arise concerning your order, we may need to contact you.

Mail this order form to the Mail Center at one of these addresses:

Insight for Living
Post Office Box 69000, Anaheim, CA 92817-0900

Insight for Living, Inc.
GPO Box 2823 EE, Melbourne, VIC 3001, Australia

Order Form
Canadian Residents

(Residents of the United States, Australia, and other international locations,
please use order form on reverse side.)

NTPCS represents the entire *New Testament Postcards* series in a special album cover, while NTP 1–3 are the individual tapes included in the series. NTP represents this study guide, should you desire to order additional copies.

NTP	Study guide	$ 6.50 ea.
NTPCS	Cassette series,	24.50
	includes all individual tapes, album cover,	
	and one complimentary study guide	
NTP 1–3	Individual cassettes,	7.48 ea.
	includes messages A and B	

Product Code	Product Description	Quantity	Unit Price	Total
			$	$

	Subtotal	
	Add 7% GST	
	British Columbia Residents *Add 7% sales tax on individual tapes or cassette series.*	
	Shipping *Shipping and handling must be added. See chart for charges.*	
	Gift to Insight for Living Ministries *Tax-deductible in Canada.*	
	Total Amount Due *Please do not send cash.*	$

Amount of Order	Canada Post
Orders to $10.00	2.00
$10.01 to 30.00	3.50
$30.01 to 50.00	5.00
$50.01 to 99.99	7.00
$100 and over	Free

Loomis Courier is also available.
Please call for details.

Prices are subject to change without notice.

Payment by: ❑ Cheque or money order payable to Insight for Living Ministries
❑ Credit card

(Circle one): Visa   MasterCard   Number _____

Expiration Date _____   Signature _____
We cannot process your credit card purchase without your signature.

Name _____

Address _____

City _____ Province _____

Postal Code _____ Country _____

Telephone (_____) _____ Radio Station ____ ____ ____ ____
If questions arise concerning your order, we may need to contact you.

Mail this order form to the Processing Services Department at the following address:

Insight for Living Ministries
Post Office Box 2510
Vancouver, BC, Canada V6B 3W7